I0480397

Day Trading Cryptocurrency

Strategies, Tactics, Mindset, and Tools Required To Build Your New Income Stream

Phil C. Senior

Day Trading Cryptocurrency

Bluesource And Friends

This book is brought to you by Bluesource And Friends, a happy book publishing company.

Our motto is **"Happiness Within Pages"**

We promise to deliver amazing value to readers with our books.

We also appreciate honest book reviews from our readers.

Connect with us on our Facebook page www.facebook.com/bluesourceandfriends and stay tuned to our latest book promotions and free giveaways.

Day Trading Cryptocurrency

Table of Contents

Day Trading Cryptocurrency

Introduction

Cryptocurrencies have become all the rage with many investors these days. In fact, the crypto hype peaked around 2017 when the price of Bitcoin rose by a scarcely believable 1,318%. The funny thing is that Bitcoin's rise was probably the smallest. Alternate currencies such as Ripple rose by an astonishing 36,018% during this period (Saifedean Ammous, 2018).

Unfortunately for many investors, the bubble burst and many people were left holding the bag right at the peak of the market. The subsequent declines convinced many of them that cryptocurrencies were highly speculative and that they were somehow fraudulent.

This point of view is held by many people across the financial industry and government. In many ways, these views only reinforce why cryptocurrencies are here to stay and why they have real value. However, as someone who's looking to day trade cryptos, you don't need to worry about the long term prospects of these currencies.

Day Trading Cryptocurrency

Day trading is a form of speculation and by its very nature, speculation seeks to take advantage of short term moves in a financial instrument. The great news for day traders is that there are so many cryptos out there right now to get started with almost instantly. All you need is a working Internet connection and you're good to go!

Having said that, getting started with day trading and executing it successfully are two different things entirely. For starters, day trading has been around for a long time but very few people manage to practice it successfully. One survey conducted by a broker indicated that 90% of people who open their account end up losing everything within 12 months (Saifedean Ammous, 2018).

Such statistics are sobering for the new day trader. I'm here to show you why these statistics won't matter for you. It's not a huge secret of any kind. It has to do with the kind of instruments most of these unsuccessful traders speculate in.

Why Day Trade Cryptos?

The average losing trader opens an account with traditional brokers and begins to trade the most widely-available financial instruments. Things such as stocks, options, and Forex (FX) currency pairs are the instruments of choice for most traders. While these instruments are easy to access, the problem is that there are millions of other traders speculating in them at the same time.

When a large number of traders speculate in a single type of instrument, that instrument becomes tough to trade. This happens because there's far too much information about it. Even worse, the most popular trading strategies and indicators won't work because everyone's using them all at once. This reduces the efficacy or the edge that the strategy has.

As a result, traders spend most of their time catching up to the market. They need to constantly evolve their trading strategies, and automating their trading strategy is impossible because they become obsolete within a matter of a few days. Think of it as opening a business in an extremely crowded niche.

If you open a clothing store on a street that already has hundreds of them, your odds of success are going to be low. There's just too much competition. Instead, if you opened it on a street that offers high foot traffic and low competition, you'll do a lot better even if you're less skilled than the person operating in the previous location.

Volatility

One of the reasons why many traders stay away from cryptos is due to their volatility. This is a bit odd because it's a lot like a businessperson saying they're trying to stay away from money. Volatility can harm you, but only if you don't know how to manage it well. There's no denying that volatility causes weird price swings now and then.

However, volatility is what moves prices to extreme levels. It's what creates quick profits for traders. Would you rather go somewhere on a bicycle that averages a mile an hour or would you rather go there in a car that averages 70 miles per hour? The choice is obvious.

The speed with which the car moves is a lot faster but as long as you drive it well, you'll get there quicker. This is what cryptos do for you. They take you to your profit targets quickly because they're volatile. Another reason for their volatility has to do with the relatively low levels of competition when it comes to trading them.

Day Trading Cryptocurrency

Thanks to the relatively low number of traders operating in them, you'll find that cryptos will move a lot faster. Thus, the earlier point about low competition assists you once again. It means you'll make more money faster.

Of course, this is easier said than done. You will need to master many skills along the way, but this is what you're going to learn in this book. There are many ways to trade crypto successfully and I'm going to show you just a few. Once you've gained experience trading them, you'll be able to figure out new strategies for yourself.

The key for you to remember is that there is no perfect strategy. You're not going to be able to win all the time. Instead, you need to ensure that you make more money than you lose whenever you do win. This is a mindset shift that many prospective day traders never make.

You're going to learn this and many more skills in this book. Practice them rigorously and you'll find money and profits flowing to you easily. Let's now move forward and take a look at the world of cryptocurrencies.

Chapter 1: Crypto 101

Before diving into how to trade cryptocurrencies, it's important for you to understand how they work. More specifically, you might be wondering what they even are. This chapter is going to give you everything you need to know in this regard.

To understand cryptocurrencies, we need to move back and first understand what money is. Simply put, money is a form of trade and is legal tender on the basis of which all trade occurs. The dollar bill in your pocket gains its value simply because everyone accepts it as a legal basis of transactions.

Money evolved due to the complexities that arose from the barter system. Bartering occurs when one person exchanges what they have for something that someone else has. A farmer might exchange sacks of rice for bundles of clothes from a cloth merchant. The barter system has a major flaw in that both parties must want what the other has.

If the cloth merchant wants wheat and not rice, the farmer is out of luck. Money evolved to erase such problems and the earliest forms of money were metals such as gold, silver, copper, and bronze. These metals had inherent value since they were used to produce more goods or were widely accepted as being valuable.

Until 1973, the world's economies tied their currencies to gold. This meant that a country could print only as many currency notes as the gold deposits they had in their vaults. This gave paper money, or fiat currency, true value. However, after the move away from the gold standard in 1973, governments were now free to print money as much as they wanted (*What Is the Gold Standard?*, 2019).

The United States and the United Kingdom had in fact moved away from the gold standard as early as 1931 and 1933, respectively. The U.S. government went so far as to seize all gold deposits belonging to citizens due to the problems gold hoarding was causing to the value of the U.S. dollar.

This is just one instance of legalized thuggery that governments have practiced over the years and it forms the basis of cryptocurrencies' existence. The problem with fiat currencies is that they're rigidly controlled by governments and political systems around the world. These entities don't have their people's best interests for the most part.

While people in the developed world have access to legal systems, large parts of the world aren't as concerned with due processes or with protecting the rights of their citizens. In fact, over three billion of the world's population has no access to banking or paper money (*What Is the Gold Standard?*, 2019).

That's over half of the world's population. Cryptocurrencies remove governments and their middlemen from the picture and give people everywhere the ability to control their own financial destiny. This is the basis of cryptocurrencies no matter what their secondary aims might be.

Day Trading Cryptocurrency

The first popular cryptocurrency was Bitcoin. Bitcoin arose from the depths of the financial crisis and, to this day, no one really knows who developed this currency. Given the negative mood prevalent in much of the developed world at the time, there was demand for Bitcoin or alternative forms of money that didn't involve banks, brokers, and governments.

Bitcoin's biggest draw was the fact that it was based on a technology called the "blockchain". The blockchain is nothing short of a revolutionary leap in terms of data security and it is being widely adopted by a variety of institutions. It's important to note that blockchain is not a cryptocurrency.

Think of it this way: If you want to cook something, you're going to have to use heat (or cold in some cases). You can cook whatever you want in any method you choose, but at some point, you'll need to apply heat. Heat is what the blockchain is and the dish you create is a cryptocurrency.

Crypto creators can add a variety of features to give each currency different flavors and textures but all of them are based on the blockchain, since the technology is fundamental to how cryptos work. Blockchain has actually been around for a long time—at least since the early nineties when computing started becoming more powerful.

However, Bitcoin was the first proof that blockchain could actually work in the real world and that it was a safe way to store information. The specifics of how blockchain works is not important for you to understand. Beyond understanding a few basics, you don't need to be a technological genius to figure out how it's used to store your crypto money.

Myths Debunked

There are close to 1,600 cryptocurrencies out there and all of them are generated through a process called "mining". Don't confuse this with physical mining which involves digging the ground up for precious metal. Crypto mining involves completing a series of tasks that reward the user with a coin or equivalent currency.

In the case of Bitcoin, the mining process involves computers deciphering complex mathematical problems and other issues. In the early days, the problems and computing power that were present were low and due to no one else being present (relatively speaking), users were rewarded with full Bitcoins.

These days, mining a single Bitcoin takes an extremely long time thanks to the high value of a single coin and the number of miners present. However, alternative cryptocurrencies, called altcoins, offer different ways of generating cryptos. Thus, cryptocurrencies offer people a way to literally create money. All you need is a computer that is powerful enough to decipher problems, connect to the network, and you're good to go.

It might take time but this is a path that many people have adopted. These days, it makes sense to mine altcoins. The bigger currencies are better off being traded or bought for the long term. As a daytrader, you don't need to worry about mining coins. It's a path that you can take if you wish, of course. However, mining doesn't have much to do with trading.

Like most of the crypto world, mining is plagued by rumors and myths. Let's take a look at some of the more popular myths surrounding cryptocurrencies.

Day Trading Cryptocurrency

Only Criminals Use It

This is an argument that has gained a lot of credibility due to governments around the world constantly pushing it. After all, why would they ever support a system that undermines their control? There's no denying that cryptos can be used for illegal purposes. One of the most notorious uses of cryptocurrencies was to launder money through websites such as Silk Road.

This website guaranteed purchase anonymity and it led to drug dealers and the like cashing in their cryptocurrencies for hard cash. Such actions have taken place and there's no escaping the fact that the potential for harm exists. However, this can be said of pretty much anything in existence.

Paper money is used in illegal ways as well. The biggest argument surrounding this myth is that cryptos guarantee anonymity. This is not true. Bitcoin does not guarantee anonymity and neither does the blockchain. There are currencies that are built on the blockchain that do this, but it's an additional feature.

It's a bit like saying that knives are dangerous because you could use them to harm people. Does it make sense to ban knives and all sharp objects? Of course not! Yet, this is what governments and bankers around the world argue about. Most bankers are in fact lying when they claim that cryptos are harmful.

The CEO of JP Morgan Chase, James Dimon, made a comment about how Bitcoin was fraudulent in 2018. The price of Bitcoin fell around 63% after this. It fell not due to Dimon's comment, but due to the fact that it had been bid upwards in a frenzy and was massively being speculated on.

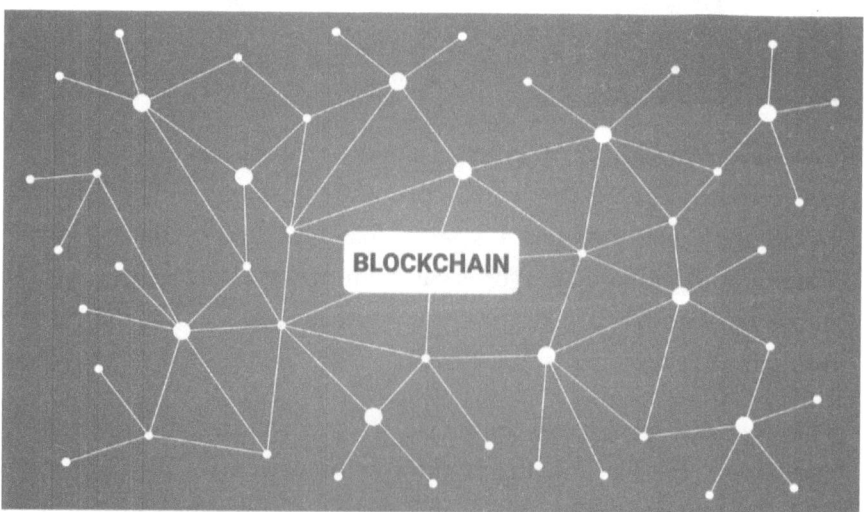

Once the price fell, what did Dimon's bank do? They went ahead and bought Bitcoin for their clients, with the other investment banks doing the same thing (Saifedean Ammous, 2018). Similarly, George Soros proclaimed at the World Economic Forum at Davos that Bitcoin was overvalued and that it wasn't a real asset. A few weeks later, it emerged that Soros had given his family office the green light to purchase Bitcoin for his portfolio.

Trusting bankers and governments to do the right thing has never been a good strategy. Let go of this myth and understand that cryptos are just a tool of exchange. The people calling it fraudulent are simply lying for the most part.

All Cryptos Offer Anonymity

This ties back to the previous myth and hopefully you now understand that blockchain and cryptos don't offer any special anonymity. There are currencies such as Monero that offer this feature, but it's an add-on that is particular to that currency.

Day Trading Cryptocurrency

Bitcoin Equals Blockchain

This is an understandable myth because Bitcoin was the first widely-used application that was built on the blockchain. However, as I explained previously, Bitcoin is simply a creation that exists on the blockchain. Blockchain is the technology and it is different from the currencies that reside on it.

Blockchain is being used in a wide variety of situations these days. Stock exchanges are moving their records to the blockchain and contracts are being generated using the technology. The financial sector has been one of the early adopters of blockchain, thanks to the sensitivity of the transactions they handle.

Day Trading Cryptocurrency

Again, blockchain does not offer anonymity. It's an alternative scheme of data storage that makes it close to impervious to hacks and other forms of data fraud.

Cryptos Can Vanish Overnight

This fear has its roots in the early days of Bitcoin. One of the issues that plagues any new market or asset is that everyone figures out what it means and how it works as time goes on. During the early days of Facebook, the company openly used its users' data in ways that would now be considered fraudulent.

This wasn't because the company was evil or unethical. It's because no one knew the true extent of such actions. When cryptos first emerged, exchanges that allowed people to buy Bitcoin and altcoins popped up. With every new trend, there is an element of speculation and this gives true frauds an easy way to take advantage of gullible people.

The first frauds that emerged were running exchanges. These exchanges offered to store people's Bitcoins for them while allowing them to speculate on prices. These days, such actions are considered criminal and no one would even consider storing their coins with a third party such as an exchange.

However, people just didn't know back then. To be fair, the exchanges that were involved in subsequent messes weren't frauds. They were merely incompetent. This led to many people losing their coins and losing a large part of their unrealized net worth.

The true frauds emerged when a wave of new altcoins began to be created. A lot of these were simple multi-level marketing scams. Some of them bordered on the ridiculous. A popular scam was OneCoin, which still exists as a husk of itself.

This was promoted by a self-proclaimed doctor, Dr. Ruja Ignatova, who had apparently worked for some of the world's biggest firms. She ran a pyramid scheme with her brother and managed to pump the value of OneCoin to a few thousand dollars. She vanished one night without a trace and is yet to be caught.

Meanwhile, the people who are still holding onto their OneCoin speculate that governments have banded together to kidnap Dr. Ruja and that she's being held hostage somewhere.

Such scams can be common but it's pretty simple to avoid them. Sticking to the established currencies and trading with the big exchanges will allow you to steer clear of such messes. The reason people fall for such a scam is due to the get-rich-quick mentality. It is possible to get rich quickly. However, don't make the mistake of chasing it.

Instead, work to develop a system that makes you money and execute it. You can't get rich by keeping an eye on the scoreboard. You need to execute your process and the result is money. Trading cryptocurrencies is no different.

Risks

Day Trading Cryptocurrency

There are a few genuine risks attached to trading cryptocurrencies. Keep these in mind before jumping into the space. All of them are avoidable and you should do your best to make sure you do.

Hype

This is the biggest risk of them all. Cryptocurrencies can be massively hyped, and this causes newbie traders to jump in with the hopes of making a quick buck. I'd like to point out that the get-rich-quick type of thinking is what creates the problem here and not the cryptos themselves.

This phenomenon is present even in the stock market where news media hypes certain companies endlessly, resulting in the stock in question falling with an almighty crash. The reason people fall for hype is due to the innate psychological biases we carry within ourselves.

The bias that affects us the most is the "herd mentality". Have you ever walked down a street and seen the person in front of you look up suddenly? Or have you walked into a restaurant and witnessed everyone eating with their hands? Peer pressure or the "herd mentality" ties back to our survival instincts, and it's hard to ignore. We rely on the actions of others to inform our own.

This is a good thing when it comes to matters of survival. If you see smoke in the distance and see lots of people running away from it, there's no doubt as to what you should do. However, the flip side is that if you see everyone jumping into a particular stock of cryptocurrency, you'll want to do the same despite it having nothing to do with your survival.

The fear of missing out compels you to invest even when you know nothing about that asset or how it works. It takes practice to ignore the pull of this bias. The best way to do so is to educate yourself about the way the asset works and to develop a sound trading strategy. If your strategy provides you with a good reason to enter it, then do so.

Create a rule for yourself to ensure that you'll ignore everything outside of your strategy, and you'll avoid the pull of herd mentality.

Safety

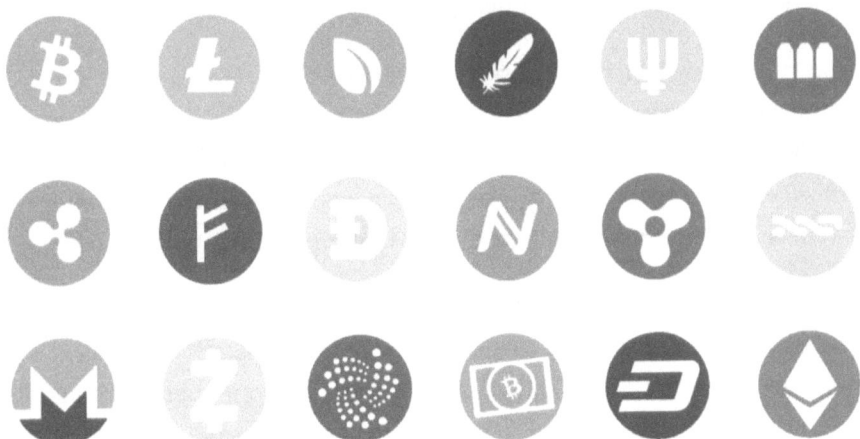

While cryptos these days are safe, there is always the possibility of a security breach. Hackers are becoming even more sophisticated than ever and cryptos are just as vulnerable as bank accounts and other data storage formats. Thanks to the blockchain, cryptos themselves are safe and no one can change their records.

However, there are vulnerabilities within the crypto ecosystem. The first is that the currency itself might be fraudulent. I've already provided an example of how charlatans can take advantage of people's desire to make money and thereby create Ponzi schemes.

This risk is avoided by sticking to well-known currencies that have been around for a while and that have been validated by the market as being sound. The second point of vulnerability is the exchange. The exchange is where you trade your cryptocurrency and these are vulnerable to hacks since their technology might not reside on the blockchain.

Day Trading Cryptocurrency

One of the most famous exchange hacks occurred with Mt. Gox back in 2013 when close to 850,000 Bitcoins were lost. While some of them were recovered, 650,000 are still missing. I'll dive into how to choose exchanges in the next chapter.

Lastly, your wallet is an important part of the security chain. In the earlier days, crypto theft was a constant risk, thanks to people using electronic wallets. You can't carry crypto around like you do paper money, but you can carry physical wallets. I'll address the issue of wallets and safeguarding your money in the next chapter.

One way of avoiding the possibility of theft from your wallet is to convert your coins back to fiat currency immediately. However, for practical purposes, you'll always have some of your trading capital in the form of cryptos, so it's best to follow good wallet-storage practices.

Volatility and Liquidity

Volatility is when the price of an asset jumps around all over the place. It is equally used to describe a situation where the price is moving in a particular direction quickly. Volatility of the latter sort is great for traders since it means you'll make money faster. The former kind of volatility is dangerous since it makes prices unpredictable.

This kind of volatility is caused by a lack of liquidity. Liquidity is a measure of how tradable an asset is. The more traders there are present for a given asset, the greater its liquidity will be. The greater the liquidity, the more prices you'll receive for your coins. Let's see how this works through an example.

Day Trading Cryptocurrency

Let's say you need to sell 100 coins, but there are just two traders in the market. These two traders will have their own opinions about what constitutes a fair price. As a result, you're not going to see too many offers for your coins beyond a certain narrow band. However, if there were a million traders in the market, the number of prices you could receive will be greater.

This means you'll receive more options if you want to buy or sell your coins. There are times when prices will narrow into a small band despite there being a large number of traders present. This occurs when an external event creates a huge impact on the market and causes prices to move in a narrow band. Such events don't last for very long but they can create losses for you.

If you're trading cryptos, you'll have to deal with volatility at some point. There are ways of mitigating this risk. Liquidity shortfalls can be avoided by trading the well-known currencies and staying away from the lesser-known ones, thereby ensuring there will always be a large market for your coins.

Taxes and Regulation

Despite cryptocurrency's aim to remove government interference from money, you'll have to deal with governments at some point. Governments love taxes and the revenues that stem from it. The lack of taxation frameworks was what pushed governments to throw a hissy fit when cryptos first emerged on the scene.

These days, crypto trading gains are taxed as normal stock trading is. Some countries are still lagging behind and don't have adequate definitions of what crypto is. As a result, their citizens don't pay any

27

taxes. While taxation means you'll have to pay money to the government on your gains, the larger risk is regulation.

Given the alternative nature of cryptocurrencies, governments could decide to make them illegal. This knee-jerk reaction was in fact followed by many governments around the world, such as India and China, where they rather naively 'banned' cryptocurrencies overnight.

Common sense prevailed and once these countries figured out how to tax them, they became 'legal' once again. Governments tend to lag behind the rest of society when it comes to adopting new methods of thinking. There's no telling how they'll react to future developments.

This risk isn't completely avoidable. The best one can do is move to reside in a country that has a stable government and trade with a reputed exchange.

Chapter 2: The Cryptocurrency Ecosystem

So how does one go about trading cryptos? To do this you'll need to interact with the rest of the crypto ecosystem. It is composed of exchanges and brokers, and you'll need to figure out how to store your coins safely using wallets. One of the advantages of trading cryptos is that you don't need to deal with brokers unless you want to.

You can trade directly with an exchange and you don't need to have a massive bank balance, either. This is not the case with stock trading, where you'll need to work for a large corporation and place trades in large volumes if you wish to trade on an exchange directly.

For most traders, trading directly with an exchange makes the most sense. There are different kinds of exchanges you can choose to trade with. All of them can be classified into one of three categories:

1. Centralized
2. Decentralized
3. Hybrid

Centralized

These exchanges tend to draw scorn from hardcore crypto-enthusiasts. In fact, these people tend to disapprove of short-term trading in cryptocurrencies as well. They're the ones who have invested in these currencies because they believe in its mission and in the changes that cryptos seek to bring about.

Whether you choose to join this crowd or not is up to you. From a trading perspective, a centralized exchange does not pose any major threat, as long as you make sure to check its validity and its reputation.

One of the reasons why centralized exchanges are viewed with scorn by the evangelist crowd is that they work in opposition to the initial aims of the cryptocurrency movement. They work just like regular stock exchanges. You open an account with them and deposit fiat currency into your account.

Once this is done, you can choose to hold your balance in the form of crypto coins or fiat currency. If you wish to trade in a particular crypto, then you buy and sell it using the platform, and that's all there is to it.

The negative aspect, according to the evangelists, is that the exchange holds your money and this poses risks. This act of holding investors' money is contrary to the aims of cryptocurrencies. After all, the point was to get rid of fiat currencies altogether, not facilitate their easy exchange and speculation in crypto.

Either way, as a trader, you don't need to worry about all of this. Just understand that centralized exchanges have a weak point in that they store your money for you. If there's a security lapse on their part or a hack of some sort, you're going to lose your money. The major centralized exchanges haven't had any issues for years and do a good job of storing data.

In addition to this, in the United States, all exchanges are regulated by the government. This adds to the overall strength of the system since the exchange company will want to preserve its good standing with the government at all costs.

Types of Instruments Offered

Almost every major exchange offers every cryptocurrency out there. Whether you need to trade all of them is besides the point. You can make a lot of money sticking to just a few currencies where the majority of volumes are concentrated.

Most exchanges offer both fiat-to-crypto pairs and crypto-to-crypto pairs. The smaller exchanges will offer the latter for the most part. Here are some of the biggest exchanges that offer fiat-to-crypto currency pairs.

- Coinbase - This is the world's largest and most popular exchange. Not only does it offer multiple cryptocurrencies, it also offers multiple fiat currencies for you to trade.
- Bittrex - This exchange is also quite popular and offers multiple cryptos but it can only be traded against the U.S. Dollar.
- Kraken - Despite the alarming name, this exchange is reliable. It used to be one of the biggest exchanges but it faced negative feedback in 2018 when they made changes to their customer service. However, they're extremely reliable and safe to trade with.
- Gemini - Much like Bittrex, this is a fast growing exchange that offers pairs with the USD.
- Robinhood - Everyone's favorite investing app also offers the ability to buy and sell cryptocurrencies. Robinhood is not the best choice for traders since it lacks a lot of the advanced

abilities that trading platforms have. However, if you want to hold onto your positions for a long time, this is a good choice.

- Bitfinex - This exchange is for serious traders and it requires a minimum of $10,000 to invest. In addition to this, you're expected to trade at a certain volume and you will be charged fees for not doing so.

Some exchanges that offer crypto-to-crypto pairs are:

- Binance - This is a fast-growing app that has a great reputation.
- KuCoin - A relatively-new player in this space but it is fast growing.

Considering the choices of instruments on offer is an important step when it comes to trading cryptos. There are other factors involved and I'll address these later in this chapter. For now, let's look at decentralized exchanges.

Decentralized

These exchanges don't play the role of a middleman when it comes to holding your funds. They simply provide you with a platform that allows you to interact with other investors and exchange your cryptos for another currency or for fiat money. This is done with smart contracts.

The specifics of these contracts aren't important from a trading perspective. This is because all of these contracts take about five days to clear and this is obviously not suitable for a day trader. As a result, I'm not going to spend time discussing these exchanges.

You'll be able to trade on the centralized exchanges or through a broker. A third option is the hybrid exchange.

Hybrid

The hybrid exchange aims to marry the advantages of both centralized and decentralized exchanges into an elegant solution. As of this writing, hybrid exchanges aren't the most popular way to trade cryptos. However, there is a lot of talk about how they are the real future of cryptocurrency trading. As of now, the most popular hybrid exchanges are Qurrex and NEXT.

Choosing an Exchange

What should you look for when evaluating an exchange? When it comes to centralized exchanges, there are a few weak points that you must evaluate. Let's take a look at these now.

Security

This is the biggest factor when it comes to deciding which exchange to trade with. Exchanges are vulnerable to hacks and other forms of shady behavior. The most common types of fraudulent behavior are pump and dump schemes. In such schemes, an operator buys a little-known or thinly-traded currency and then spreads word of how lucrative an investment it is.

Once other investors start buying it at higher prices, the operator sells their holdings and makes money. Such behavior doesn't have much to do with the exchange but it plays an important role in limiting such actors from signing onto their platforms. For starters, look at the forms and documents that the exchange requires you to furnish upon signing up.

Exchanges that need few forms will naturally attract fraudulent actors. Second, look at how they handle security. Do these exchanges offer two factor authentication? Are they regulated by a major governmental agency? In the United States, all exchanges come under the purview of the SEC and are liable to pay major penalties if they breach the rules.

Another point to verify is whether the exchange offers cold storage for your funds. Cold storage refers to your funds being stored offline so there's low risk of a hack affecting your balances. Lastly, exchanges are supposed to hold an equivalent amount of customer balances in their own bank accounts. This proof needs to be audited and verified by regulatory authorities.

Day Trading Cryptocurrency

Variety of Currencies Offered

How many currencies does the exchange offer and how easy is it to trade between fiat currencies and the cryptos on offer? This seems like a minor point but the more variety an exchange offers, the more reputed it is and the safer your money will be.

Liquidity

This is a big one. You want the exchange of your choice to have as much liquidity as possible when it comes to trading volumes. The easiest way to evaluate this is to read reviews of the exchange on popular crypto news sites and to look at volumes on coinmarketcap.com and bitcoincharts.com.

These websites give you the aggregate volumes and also break them down based on the exchange where they're being traded.

Fees

You will pay commissions on your trades unless you opt for an investing app like Robinhood. However, if you're a serious trader, you want a broker or exchange that charges fees. This way, you know your orders aren't being sold by the broker to bigger institutions. This is how apps like Robinhood make money.

Typically, the fees per trade amount are not less than 1%, with some exchanges diving as low as 0.02%. Low fees will seem attractive but don't make them your sole point of choice. Evaluate other factors as well. More secure exchanges will charge you a higher commission and this is a good thing. After all, the money is being spent on protecting your investment.

Ease of Use

Ease of use covers many things. At first glance, you'll be tempted to look at just the trading platform and how easily you can place orders. However, you also want to take into account the ease of withdrawal and how quickly you can access your funds once deposited. How many deposit and withdrawal options does the exchange provide?

In addition to this, check if there is a settlement delay on your trades and on withdrawal. Some exchanges take as long as five working days to transfer your money. In addition to this, they don't have minimum investment requirements but have minimum withdrawal requirements.

Read all of their terms and conditions carefully before opening an account. Some exchanges impose transaction limits depending on your account size, so watch out for those as well.

Customer Support

This is a big one, especially when it comes to crypto brokers. How easily can you contact their customer support division and how responsive are they? Crypto is a fast-moving area and there are always developments that require you to move quickly. You'll need responsive customer service that can quickly answer your questions about your money and its status.

Brokers

Should you use brokers to trade cryptocurrencies? From a trading standpoint, there isn't much difference between using a broker versus trading with an exchange directly. At the end of the day, you're paying someone an access fee to trade, and these fees will be pretty much the same no matter who you choose.

The advantage when it comes to using brokers is that a lot of the bigger brokers around the world are offering cryptos for trading. This makes it easy to integrate crypto day trading with your regular investing or trading. For example, many FX brokers offer crypto pairs as contracts for difference, or CFDs. These instruments are banned in the United States, so you don't need to worry about what they are.

There's also the double-edged sword that is leverage. Leverage refers to a trader borrowing money to place trades in the market. In the United States, brokers cannot offer leverage greater than 50:1. This means you cannot borrow more than $50 for every dollar you deposit in your account. This sounds like a lot and it is. When it comes to trading FX pairs, such levels of leverage are necessary to boost gains.

The downside of leverage is that it can wipe you out pretty quickly. Consider an example. Let's say you buy $1,000 worth of currencies using 50:1 leverage. This means you'll place less than $20 of your own money in the trade. If the value of your trading position increases by just 2% to $1,020, you'll earn a gain of 100%. This is because your initial investment was $20 (or close to it).

This sounds great. However, if the price of the position were to decline by the same amount (2%), you'll end up losing your entire invested capital. Leverage brings with it the promise of high reward but there's high risk attached to it. At 50:1 leverage, you'll be running high risks. This is needed when trading FX because those instruments move in very small proportions.

However, you don't need such levels of leverage when trading cryptos. You can check with a mainstream broker as to whether they allow you to invest in cryptos directly. Alternatively, you can trade crypto ETFs. ETF stands for "exchange traded fund" and it is a managed fund that invests in a certain strategy.

In the case of a crypto ETF, its managers invest fiat money into cryptocurrencies. The great thing about ETFs is that you can trade them just like you would a normal stock. This means you don't need to open a separate account to trade cryptos. You can simply make them an extension of your regular trading activities. This solves a lot of the problems that might stop a regular trader from opening an account with a crypto exchange.

The best part about using a broker is that you're almost always guaranteed a good price for your asset and you don't need to worry about liquidity. While liquidity risk is impossible to completely eliminate, many brokers reduce this risk thanks to having multiple exchanges through which they place orders.

The best way to choose a broker is to follow the same evaluation steps as previously mentioned with exchanges. Make sure the brokers are present in a highly-regulated jurisdiction and that they offer excellent customer service. In addition, make sure they offer easy withdrawal options and that their deposit minimums are low. Take a look at commissions as well.

Thanks to the highly-regulated nature of regular broking, you don't need to worry too much about the security versus brokerage fee trade-off. Simply select the broker that offers you the lowest commission. However, beware of zero-commission brokers such as Robinhood. Their platforms might not be optimized for trading and you might find that the prices you receive will be worse than normal.

Wallets and Storage

Wallets are how you'll store your cryptocurrency. Some traders don't do this and, to be honest, there's no need for you to do this as well. It applies only to traders who wish to store their capital and earnings in the form of cryptocurrency.

The traditional method in which trading works is you sign up for an account with an exchange or a broker, and then you transfer your money to them. In the case of an exchange, they'll convert your fiat currency to the crypto of your choice when you place a trade. Once you cash out of the trade, you can convert those profits into fiat currency or into an alternative currency.

You can withdraw your profits either as fiat currency or in the form of a crypto. If you choose the latter option, you'll need a place to store this money. This is what a wallet is. Keep in mind that a crypto wallet is very different from eWallets such as Apple Pay or Samsung Pay.

Those tools are simply digital fiat money. Crypto wallets are far more secure and they come in many different forms. Let's look at some of the terms associated with crypto wallets.

Jargon

There are a few terms associated with crypto storage and wallets that might confuse you. The first is the term "hot" or "cold" wallet. A hot wallet indicates storage that is connected to the internet. A cold wallet isn't connected. Your wallet has a unique address that indicates its place on the blockchain. This is the equivalent of your bank account number when referring to a fiat currency.

When someone wishes to transfer money to you, you'll provide your wallet address to them. To confirm the transfer, you will need to validate your public key. The public key is a code that is connected to your wallet address. You don't have to share this with anyone else.

Coupled to the public key is a private key that allows you to enter your wallet and view its balance or withdraw cash. Think of it as a password to your fiat banking app. To understand these terms better, let's examine how a crypto wallet works.

The wallet does not store any balances by itself. Instead, it stores the wallet's private and public keys. These keys authenticate the wallet's presence on the blockchain. When someone sends you money, they're telling the blockchain that they're pushing money from one address to another.

The blockchain then needs to validate that your address is real. It does this by using the public and private keys. Thus, the entire transaction is electronic and there's no transfer of physical money or coins.

Types of Wallets

There are different kinds of wallets you can use depending on the amount of money you wish to store as crypto. The first is an online wallet. The advantages of an online wallet are that they allow quick transactions. Your keys are stored on the company's private server and they allow you full access as long as you're connected to the internet. This is the ideal choice for traders.

The disadvantage is that you're still vulnerable to being hacked. Your wallet information is stored on the company's server and any breach in security is likely to result in a situation where you're not going to be able to do anything. If your balances are low, this is a great way to store your money.

Closely linked to online wallets are mobile wallets. These are phone apps that allow you to store your cash. They can be used to pay at merchants that accept cryptocurrencies and you can pay using QR codes, and so on. The downsides are the same as online wallets. In fact, given that your wallet is on your phone, it makes your phone an especially-prized asset. Any damage it incurs could result in your money being lost.

Third on the list is a desktop wallet. Common practice is to use the desktop wallet as a cold wallet. This means storing the wallet and keys on a computer that has never been connected to the internet. This significantly reduces any chances of being hacked. However, such computers are unlikely to be updated with software patches and are vulnerable to any malware that might be found on the wallet software itself.

Furthermore, desktop wallets make it difficult to transact and aren't a convenient choice. You'll need to transfer your coins from the cold wallet to a hot one and this opens it up for corruption. Generally speaking, desktop wallets aren't a great choice. Much like the mobile wallet, if your computer crashes, you're going to lose your coins.

One of the safest types of wallets are hardware wallets. These are electronic devices such as USB hard drives that store your information using advanced encryption. They tend to be expensive but if you have significant assets in crypto, then you need one. They aren't connected to the internet for the most part and are considered cold as a result.

The safest method of storage is a paper wallet. These are a bit difficult to understand at first, but they are actually pretty simple. To create a paper wallet, you head over to a paper wallet generator such as walletgenerator.net or bitaddress.org. You'll print out a piece of paper that has your public and private keys, along with a QR code.

The QR code contains your wallet's public address and it can be used to transfer money to you. If you wish to withdraw money, you can use the private key and withdraw funds. Since your keys are literally on a piece of paper, they cannot be hacked. However, being physical, storing them is of paramount importance.

People with significant crypto holdings lock them in safes and leave them untouched for years on end. There's a learning curve to using them but if you're carrying millions of crypto assets, then it's best for you to follow this method.

Best Practices

When choosing a wallet, there are a few things you should do to ensure the safety of your funds. At the very least, you should have one online wallet that you can use to transfer small amounts of money for your trading purposes. You should have a second wallet if your crypto assets are greater than $1,000 or more.

Hardware wallets are the best choice. You can visit coincentral.com to read about the various types of wallets out there and how the best ones compare to one another. It's critical to look at the type of asset the wallet supports.

Not all wallets support different types of currencies. Some wallets are designed for just one asset type and nothing else. Therefore, make sure you research this before purchasing anything. Another consideration is anonymity. Some wallets offer additional security in the form of anonymous transactions, and so on. These typically cost quite a lot but if you're holding five figures worth of crypto assets, they're worth the expense.

Chapter 3: Price Chart Basics

Now that you have a good idea of what cryptocurrencies are and how they work, it's time to dive in and take a look at how to trade them. The first question is: Why should you day trade them? There are other ways of trading such as swing trading, so why not opt for those instead?

The reason is that the additional volatility in cryptos gives you great returns for your time invested when day trading them. You can choose to swing trade them, of course, but this is only going to result in your money growing at a slower pace. Day trading is tougher than swing trading, but by learning the basics and practicing constantly, you'll be able to achieve success with it.

The first thing that every trader encounters is the price chart. Most beginner traders are introduced to price charts through the financial news media. These channels show prices as a straight line that dips up or down. These charts look helpful but from a trading perspective, they really aren't.

In order to understand why, we need to step back and examine what prices are. Prices are represented on a chart through time frames. For example, a 15-minute chart represents price action that occurred every 15 minutes, a daily chart shows what happened on a daily basis, and so on.

During these time intervals (let's say 15 minutes for the purposes of this example), prices move up and down and aren't stationary. A basic line chart only plots where prices ended up at the end of those 15-minute intervals. It doesn't show you what happened in between those price levels.

This is why a line chart doesn't add any value to traders. It's helpful if you wish to understand the basic contours of the market, but when it comes to trading, you'll end up missing a ton of information.

Thankfully, there's another way of representing prices.

Candlesticks

Candlesticks are an extremely old method of representing price action. They've been around since the 1600s, in fact, and are considered the best way of representing what goes on in the markets. To understand how candlesticks work, you need to learn the four components of price action.

These are the: Open, high, low, and close. Together these are referred to as OHLC. OHLC gives you a quick picture of how price behaved and, more importantly, how traders dealt with prices. Figuring out the intentions of other traders is extremely important when it comes to day trading.

A long term investor is concerned with the fundamental prospects of an asset. This is because they're looking to hold onto it for at least a decade or more. During this period, the asset will appreciate or depreciate according to its fundamentals. A company's stock price will reflect its long term earnings growth.

However, in the short term, this is not the case. When you're dealing with day trading time frames of 15 minutes and less, you're dealing with the emotions of other traders in the markets. Emotions are what drive short-term prices. Thus, trading successfully on these time frames comes down to being able to spot the direction in which momentum exists and then following that train.

This is what extremely complex looking indicators seek to do. As I mentioned in the introduction, you don't need super complex indicators to make sense of cryptos. Simple indicators work just as well. An even better way to figure out short-term momentum is to look at the shape of the price bars themselves.

When looking at candlestick charts, each price candle or price bar conveys information about what traders think is going on in the market. The way the OHLC prints contains many clues as to what's going on with the asset.

Candles

Let's look at a basic candlestick chart section. Figure 1 illustrates this.

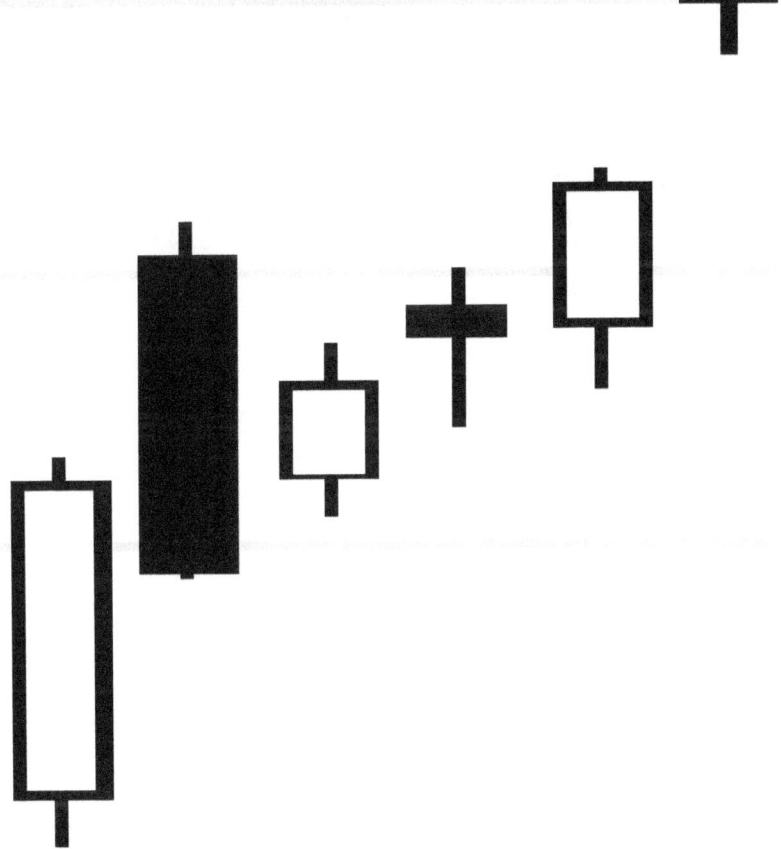

Figure 1: Candlesticks

In Figure 1,there are five full candles that you can see and a little bit of a sixth candle that is cut off on the top right. There are three bars (I'll be using bars and candles interchangeably) that are colored white and two that are colored black. All of them have different shapes and sizes as well as differently-sized lines shooting from the top and bottom.

Day Trading Cryptocurrency

The colored portion of a bar is called its body. With candlesticks, the color of the body gives us a visual representation of what happened during that interval. In this picture, each bar represents 15 minutes of price action. You can choose any color scheme of your own, but in this book, I've chosen to represent price increases by coloring the respective bars white and price decreases by coloring the bars black.

Bars that increase in price are those where the price opened at a lower level and closed at a higher one. The first bar in Figure 1 is an example of this. Such bars are called "bullish" bars. In contrast, the second bar represents a situation where prices opened at a high level and then closed lower, slightly below the close of the first bar. These bars are called "bearish" bars.

With bullish bars, the bottom of the body (not the vertical line from the bottom of the body) is the "open" and the top of the body is the "close". In a bearish bar, this order is reversed. The top of the body is the "open" and the bottom of the body is the "close". The vertical lines that are shooting from the top and bottom of the bar are the high and the low, respectively.

The "high" is the highest point that prices attained during this interval. The "low" is the lowest point they went to. In a single picture, candlesticks thus manage to convey a ton of information regarding price action. The first and most obvious thing to note is the size of the candle's body.

A large body indicates strength in whichever direction the price is moving in. Notice the difference in size between the first bar and the other bullish bars. If prices hover within a small range, leading to a small bar, then this indicates that traders pushing prices in a given direction are encountering massive resistance.

With candlesticks, it's important to look at the bigger picture and not get caught up trying to analyze individual candles. For example, the second bar in Figure 1 is a strong bearish bar. However, notice that prices tend to move upwards anyway. If you're going to look at just this bar and ignore the others, then you're going to miss the forest for the trees.

Often you'll read about the importance of analyzing each and every candle in a chart. You don't need to do this. In fact, doing this will only lead to overanalysis and you won't be able to figure out which way prices are likely to move. The best way to analyze candlesticks is to watch for patterns. These patterns will help tune you into what will likely happen next, and you can trade accordingly.

Candlestick Patterns

There are many ways of classifying candlestick patterns. Some traders choose to divide them between "bullish" and "bearish" patterns and look for these shapes to present themselves. The best way to trade candlesticks is to look for board-based patterns that give you the best clue for underlying price action.

Order flow is what causes prices to move in certain ways. By looking for the telltale signs of order flow changes, you'll be able to align yourself with the direction that prices will most likely move in. Patterns by themselves are pretty powerful when it comes to figuring out this direction.

However, they're extremely powerful when you combine them with trend/range analysis, support levels, and resistance levels. You'll learn more about these in the next two chapters. For now, let's move forward and look at a few powerful candlestick patterns that will help you decode price action.

Inside Bars

Inside bars are a two-bar pattern. They can indicate either a continuation of the existing move or a reversal. A continuation occurs when there is no significant support or resistance level in sight, while a reversal occurs close to a strong support or resistance level.

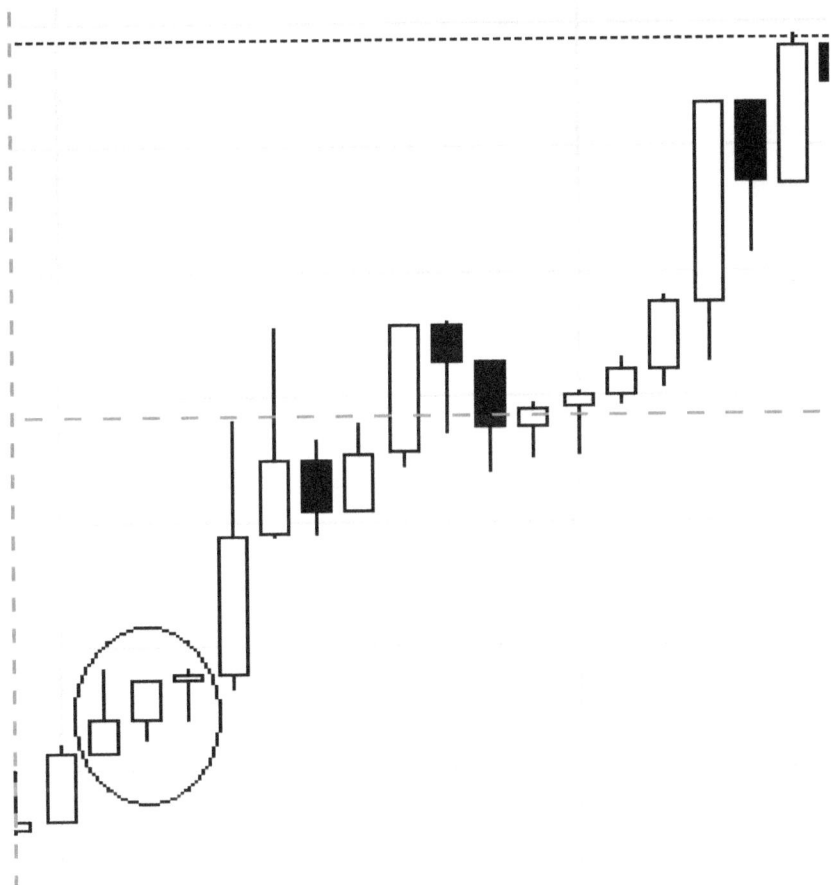

Figure 2: Inside Bars on Bitcoin

Figure 2 indicates an inside bar formation that represents a continuation pattern. In this instance, the inside bar formation consists of three bars. This is a common occurrence that makes the pattern even more powerful. Notice how the two bars on the right (within the circled area) are contained within the first bar.

The first bar isn't a particularly strong one. In fact, it has a significant wick above it. By itself, this single bar can be considered a bearish indication. As explained earlier, bearish patterns indicate that prices are likely to move downwards while bullish ones indicate the possibility of prices moving up.

However, as the subsequent bars print, we see an inside-bar formation. Why is this formation powerful? For starters, a bar contained within the previous bar's range means that the traders representing the other side of the market could not push prices back down. In fact, it shows that the bulls (in the case of Figure 2) were able to maintain prices despite the bears trying to push back.

We already know that the bears are present thanks to the formation of the first bar. The fact they could not follow through and that the bulls still managed to hold prices to these levels indicates serious strength. In this case, BTC (Bitcoin) explodes upwards and a major uptrend is established.

More often than not, you'll see prices continue to hang around these levels before exploding upwards. No pattern is perfect, so you're not going to see instant price explosions as is the case in Figure 2. If they do occur, then hold on for as long as possible. If the formation circled in Figure 2 happened to occur near a strong resistance level, then we would have likely seen prices move downwards. That's how a reversal pattern plays out.

A lot of traders are aware of inside bars but few manage to make money with them. Why is this so? It goes back to interpreting price action. A lot of traders look to trade in geometric ways. What I mean is that they search for fancy shapes on a chart and think that this is what represents true price action.

This is not the case. A shape is just a shape. The formation by itself means nothing unless underlying order flow backs it up. This is why it's extremely important that you look for inside bars when a trend is already in place. The best place to look for them is in the beginning of trends.

You'll learn more about identifying trends in the next chapter. Keep in mind that you will see a lot of inside-bars print during environments that are the opposite of trends (ranges). The reason why traders lose money with this formation is because they look to trade this pattern in the wrong environment.

A trend is the correct environment for the inside bar, so always remember this: If a strong support or resistance level is present close by, then it's likely going to indicate a reversal. If there isn't one, then it most likely indicates a continuation.

Pin Bars

Pin bars are an extremely easy pattern to spot and they also happen to be very powerful. When combined with support and resistance levels, they predict the direction of prices with great accuracy. Unlike inside bars that can indicate either reversal or continuation, pin bars are exclusively reversal signals. Prices will always reverse their current direction when a pin bar is printed.

Day Trading Cryptocurrency

Figure 3: Pin Bar on BTC

Figure 3 is a 15-minute chart of BTC. The pin bar is marked by the oval. Notice how prices trend downwards and then bounce upwards immediately after the pin bar is printed. Pin bars happen to be pretty easy to spot. They have long tails, or wicks, and small bodies.

As a rule of thumb, you want the tail or wick to be at least three times as large as the body. A bar that has a long tail is a bullish signal. One with a long wick (above the body) is a bearish signal. The color of the pin bar's body doesn't matter. What's more important is that the bar signals a reversal of existing price action.

Notice in Figure 3 that the price of BTC was declining sharply and the pin indicated a bullish reversal. The best pins can be found at the end of a trend, or when the trend takes a bit of a breather and moves sideways for a bit. In addition to this, a pin that has its tail or wick hit a significant support or resistance level will almost always result in a reversal.

A word of caution when it comes to pin bars: Often, traders will fall into the trap of thinking that pins are magical formations. They'll see an asset decline in price for a long period of time and will spot a single bullish pin bar. On the strength of that single pin bar, they'll decide to buy the asset (go long) and will usually end up making a loss.

This is an unintelligent way to trade. You need to take market context into account before placing trades. Remember that a single formation doesn't indicate a turn in the direction of price. In the above example, the pin bar is formed at significant support and the bear trend has been showing signs of slowing down for a while.

These factors aren't shown in the interests of conserving space. You'll learn about spotting them in the next two chapters. For now, keep in mind that it's important to look at the overall context of the market before placing trades in a given direction. The shape of the pattern is just one input in this decision.

Engulfing Bars

An engulfing bar is also called an "outside bar" by some traders. Like pin bars, this is a powerful reversal pattern. The difference between an engulfing bar and a pin bar is that they tend to occur right at the end of a trend. Pin bars can occur at the end of trends as well as in the middle of them when a trend moves sideways to catch a breather before continuing in its given direction.

Engulfing bars occur right when a new trend is about to begin. As a result, you'll often see them forming in large sideways movements. If you spot an engulfing bar formation near an important support or resistance level, you can be certain that prices are about to move significantly in the direction suggested by the engulfing bar.

Figure 4: Engulfing Bar in BTC

Figure 4 shows an engulfing bar formation in the chart of Bitcoin. Notice how far BTC fell after the formation. Also notice how the uptrend to the left of the chart moves into a small sideways movement before plunging downwards in a downtrend. This highlights a major difference between trading cryptos and regular financial instruments.

This sort of price action will usually not occur in stocks or FX. You'll typically see long uptrends, followed by longer sideways moves before the trend changes direction. The chart in Figure 4 is a one hour chart and the sideways move at the top of the uptrend lasted for two days at the most.

Contrast this with the FX market where sideways moves forming at the end of trends last for months on end. Also notice how short and sharp the trends are. This is an illustration of the volatility you will find when trading cryptos. The downtrend only lasts for a few hours but it moves a long way.

This means you need to pull the trigger without hesitation on entry because the chances of getting in later in the trend will be close to non-existent. Notice how BTC does not give you any other chances to get in once the trend gets going. It exhausts itself and then moves in another sideways pattern, which indicates that an upswing might occur shortly.

Coming back to the engulfing bar, you can see that the pattern consists of at least two bars. Much like the inside bar, the more bars that are engulfed, the stronger the pattern is. The color of the bar on the right indicates the trade direction.

Entering using an engulfing bar is a bit tricky because some of them can be quite large. In the case of an inside bar, you can enter once the price moves below the extent of the bigger bar and place your stop loss above the smaller bar. With pin bars, you can enter on the close of the pin bar with the stop above the high or the low. With engulfing bars, placing your stop above the extent of the outside bar and entering on its close might create too much of a gap between the entry and stop loss.

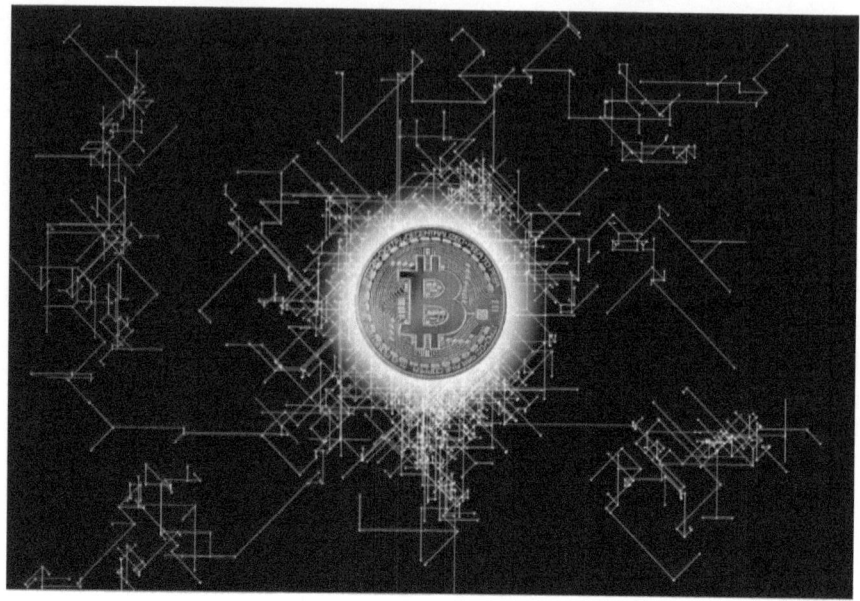

As a result, your trade will have to move a long distance in order to make money. A solution for this is to wait for the next bar to move lower than the outside bar and place a stop loss order near the halfway point of the outside bar. This brings your profit target a lot closer and increases the probability of your trade working out.

Something to point out is that you need to watch for this formation only when trends are coming to an end. In addition, you want them to form near the boundaries of sideways moves. Often, you'll see these patterns forming in the middle of the sideways move. These are not valid patterns, since from an order flow perspective, they don't mean anything.

What's happening in this price-action pattern is that the traders who are backing the new trend are overwhelming the traders pushing the old trend, and are literally engulfing their orders. This is why the big bar is so crucial. It overshadows everything that came before it and indicates that strength has moved from one side of the market to the other.

These three patterns will help you trade in pretty much any market out there. They're extremely powerful and will help you align yourself with the path of least resistance. Best of all, they're pretty simple to spot. The challenge for you as a trader is to sift the valid signals from the invalid ones.

Paying attention to the market's context will help you do this. This is what you're going to learn in the next chapter.

Chapter 4: Trends and Ranges

The market will move in two ways, broadly speaking. It will either move in a particular direction or it will move sideways. A market that has a directional bias to it is said to be trending. A sideways market is said to be ranging, or in a range. Ranges are far more common than trends.

This means that you'll be placing trades in sideways moves for the most part. This is also what makes trading particularly challenging. If the market doesn't move in any direction, how can you make money? Price action patterns can help you locate ideal entry opportunities.

However, you'll be able to figure out which opportunities are the best by paying attention to the way in which the market is behaving or has behaved. This is why trend versus range analysis is so important. The good news is that, thanks to the relatively-lower competition in the crypto space, spotting opportunities is a lot easier.

In the FX or stock market, you're going to have to compete against extremely sophisticated traders, and this skews price movements to a large extent. As a result, you'll end up taking trade entries that don't necessarily make sense. The first step to deciphering what's going on in the market is to look at what kind of ranges are being formed.

Ranges

Day Trading Cryptocurrency

A range is a sideways movement in price. Even a small sideways move of two or three bars counts as a range. It might not be significant but it is a range nonetheless. Ranges form for two reasons: The first reason is that the traders pushing the trend might be taking a breather. The second reason is that the counter-trend traders might be overcoming those pushing the trend.

The second type of range is far easier to trade. This is because they tend to be larger in size and their non-directional nature will be easy to spot. Typically, these ranges are preceded by what is called "exhaustion". Exhaustion is when a trend literally exhausts itself in a large push and comes to an end. You'll learn more about exhaustion shortly.

The ranges that form in the middle of trends can be trickier to trade. During the initial portions of a trend, the ranges that are formed will be small in size and will hardly register as being ranges. You might see prices move sideways for two or three bars before continuing in the direction of the trend.

However, as the trend progresses, you'll see that the ranges become bigger in size and they'll even move against the trend. The other wrinkle that occurs is that these ranges won't be perfectly sideways all the time. For the most part, they will have a mild directional bias to them that confuses traders.

Types of Ranges

Bitcoin / U.S. Dollar · 15 · BITFINEX   ●   O9440.0 H9450.0 L9427.7 C9450.0 +10.1 (+0.11%)

Figure 5: Range Types

Figure 5 illustrates how ranges change as trends evolve. This is a 15-minute chart of BTC. It depicts an uptrend that eventually comes to an end. There are two instances of price action patterns indicating the end of this uptrend. Can you spot them? Hint: They're both engulfing bar patterns.

Coming back to ranges, you can see four ranges marked with the labels 1, 2, 3 and 4. The first range is comically small compared to the next three. This sequence also illustrates how crypto trends move in the smaller time frames. In a normal FX trend, you might see up to eight or nine ranges of varying sizes.

In those trends, the size of the ranges keep changing as well. You might see a small range print after a larger one, which often confuses new traders. With cryptos, the price action is a lot cleaner. It's just another advantage of trading cryptos. Coming back to the chart, notice that range 1 is pretty small.

This is a range at the start of the uptrend. There is hardly any bearish pressure and as a result, the bulls are merely taking a breather in this range. Prices start climbing upwards until it hits range 2. Here, the bears assert themselves a bit more. This is evident by both the size of the range (compared to range 1) as well as the degree to which the bears push back into the trend.

Notice how prices make a new high before being pushed down by the bears in range 2. This is a clear indication that the bears are returning in force. Prices continue upwards until we reach range 3. This is the biggest one of them all and you can see how every bullish push is countered by a bearish one. However, the bulls are still strong and hold the upper hand in this market.

They push prices higher and prices explode. Notice how the bars increase in size. Eventually, they exhaust themselves and this gives rise to the final range, which is the largest. It's big in terms of boundaries (from top to bottom) as well as individual bar sizes.

The bars in them are huge, and this is indicative of the bears overcoming the bulls steadily. There are two engulfing bars printed within this range, one in the beginning and one in the middle, both of them close to the range boundary on top. This further increases the case for a bearish entry. Eventually, prices make their way down.

So how can you combine price action patterns with range analysis? For starters, the direction of prices tells you that you should be looking only for bullish entries. You can trade against the trend but this is a bit like walking up on the down escalator. Why would you want to make things harder for yourself?

This means you should be looking for bullish price action patterns. If you spot a bearish pin bar or an engulfer outside of the large range, these are invalid patterns. The best place to spot possible entries into the trend is to look for them in the ranges. Notice that the ranges have patterns printing within them.

There is a pin bar that prints within range 2 as well as a pin that prints just before the range. Range 3 has a pin bar within it as well as a bullish engulfing bar that prints just outside the range. In addition to this, there are inside bars printing all over the chart.

Take care with trading inside bars within a range. As mentioned in the previous chapter, you should be trading inside bars only within trending portions of price. Within a range, price action can be chaotic, so an inside bar isn't as powerful. Even with pins and engulfing bars, take care to trade the ones that print near the range boundaries.

Trend Analysis

Analyzing trends is a lot easier than ranges. For starters, all of the price action that you see in Figure 5 is an example of a trend. Traders often think of trends and ranges as being an either/or proposition. This is not the case.

Day Trading Cryptocurrency

As you can see, ranges occur within trends all the time. The mistake traders make is to think of the bits between ranges as being trends. These can be thought of as being the trending portions of a trend, but they aren't a trend by themselves.

Spotting a trend is pretty easy. As long as there's a bias to the price movement, a trend is on. Often, ranges will have a directional bias to them. In such cases, they'll tell you the direction of the trend they belong to. When you look at a price chart, your first step should be to figure out the trend and range characteristics of it.

Much like how Figure 5 has been broken down, you'll need to mark the relevant ranges and the quality of the trending portions. The best way to look at the quality of the trending portions is to measure the distance they manage to cover. Going back to Figure 5, notice that the extent of the trending move between boxes 2 and 3 is a lot smaller than the one between boxes 3 and 4.

The largest push comes after box 4, and this is an exhaustive move. How can you spot these? For starters, look at the size of the bullish bars. They expand to a completely new level. This happens after you know that bears are increasing their presence in the market (thanks to looking at range 4 and the way in which ranges have progressed thus far).

This indicates that the bulls are looking to seriously press their case and assert themselves. However, they're doing this against significant bearish pressure. They move prices to such an extent that the upswing becomes almost vertical. This is an unsustainable rate at which one can push prices and it results in the bears pushing back. This prints as an engulfing bar.

Notice on the engulfer how long its wick is. This indicates that bulls pushed prices that high before the bears had enough and pushed back down. The presence of tails or wicks is a sign that the trend traders have extended themselves too much. Combine this with the presence of unsustainable price angle and the increasing presence of bears and we have a case for exhaustion.

Another telltale sign is the size of the engulfing bar. Notice how it's much bigger than anything the bulls have produced thus far. Its size is at least 1.5 times the biggest bullish bar in the trend. Thus, the context in which price is moving tells us everything we need to know.

Once exhaustion occurs, you can be certain that the range that prints after it will be one where the balance of the market is being redistributed. In this case, the bears are taking over from the bulls. Within range 5, notice how the bearish bars are a lot bigger than the bullish ones.

The relative size of the bars will often point to who has greater control in the markets. Pay attention to these when you trade and you'll be able to figure out what the market's context is.

Trading Without Patterns

Once you become good at identifying the price action context the market is in, you'll find that trading becomes a lot easier and will involve far less guesswork. You won't have to worry about how your trade will turn out or whether the pattern you've identified is a clean one.

In fact, you'll be able to trade without the assistance of any patterns. Consider Figure 5 once again. As long as you know that the ranges printing in that uptrend are not the type that print at the end of a trend, the direction in which price will eventually head is obvious. You can choose to enter at a price that is close to a range bottom with a stop loss slightly below that and then hold on until you spot exhaustion.

Once you do spot exhaustion, you can short the instrument and wait for the price to move downwards. This is how professional traders trade. They don't use indicators or anything fancy. All the information you need is right there on the price chart. Many traders are hesitant to trade in this way.

There's a good reason for this and it has everything to do with the mindset they carry within them. They expect trading entries to be accompanied with a ton of indicators that confirm that their decision is correct. Unfortunately, trading doesn't work this way. You'll never know whether your entry is going to work out.

You'll learn more about this in the chapter on risk management. No matter how great your system is or how amazing an indicator is, there will be times when it will be wrong. The presence of a candlestick pattern doesn't provide you with any more indication that a trade will work than the weather does.

In order to trade successfully, you need to read the underlying price action and then align yourself with its flow. The purpose of studying candlestick patterns is to be able to figure out the underlying order flow. Patterns are an easy way to shortcut the process of figuring out what's going on in the markets.

They don't create order flow by themselves. This is why many traders lose money. They expect that the mere presence of a pattern will guarantee success, all the while ignoring the broader price action context. Trend and range analysis will give you a leg up on your competition because most of them are busy looking for geometric shapes on a chart.

Master trend and range analysis and you'll be trading like a professional and making real money.

Chapter 5: Support and Resistance

Trend and range analysis is an important part of trading, but analyzing support versus resistance is just as important. Support and resistance levels are a slightly misunderstood concept in technical analysis. Most traders tend to think of them as being simple lines on a chart.

Instead of thinking of them like this, it's far better to consider how they come to be from an order flow perspective. The market for any instrument is composed of a variety of traders placing orders, bidding, and offering their holdings to the market. These traders keep a close eye on price levels. There are some traders who have the ability to influence prices to a greater degree than others.

No trader can control or corner a market. Even smaller markets such as crypto are far too large for this to be a profitable strategy. When a trader attempts to corner a market, they have to borrow money, and as a result, everyone else in the market starts squeezing prices against them.

However, there is a lot of profit to be made in influencing prices for a small amount of time. I'm not talking about price manipulation when I mention influencing. I'm talking about buying or selling large quantities that are enough to move markets in a particular direction.

When the larger traders do this, they create areas on the chart that attract other traders in the belief that price action in these zones is going to be more predictable than in others. As a result, these zones become powerful enough to influence the way prices behave. This is the essence of what a support or resistance zone is.

A support zone is one where prices are literally supported. Price often bounces off these zones and either moves higher or holds above them. A resistance zone is one that limits the rise of prices. They spend some time at this level before either breaking past it or turning back downwards.

The thing that confuses a lot of traders about support and resistance zones is that they often change character. What I mean is that a broken support level will often turn into a resistance when prices test the level from below. Similarly, a resistance level will turn into a support level once prices break past above it.

There are a few things you should keep in mind when identifying support and resistance zones.

Swing Points

The most common type of support or resistance zones are prior swing points. As prices seek to test them from above or below, the nature of the previous swing will clue you in to how strong the level is and how likely it is to hold.

In case you're wondering what a swing point is, it's literally a place on the chart where price changes direction.

Day Trading Cryptocurrency

Figure 6: Swing Points

Figure 6 illustrates three swing points in an uptrend in BTC. Notice how prices move away from the point with some force. Do not confuse swing points with sideways moves. Prices will often hang around a level for a while before changing direction. These zones are not swing points.

They're a different type of support and resistance level and can be traded, but don't evaluate their strength like you would swing points. There are few ways in which you can figure out how strong a prior swing point is.

Angles

Take note of the angle at which price moves into the level and the angle at which it moves away from it. This is a great way to evaluate the level. If it moves away at a steeper angle than the one with which it approached the level, then you can rest assured that the traders lurking there are strong.

The first swing point on the left in Figure 6 is an example of a strong swing point as is the final one. Notice how price hits these zones in a horizontal manner and leaves in an extremely forceful manner.

Also notice how prices don't hang around there too long. At the most, you'll see two bars printing to form a swing point. This is a key differentiator between a swing point and a spot where price moves sideways.

Relative Sizes

Another way to examine the strength of a swing point is to look at the size of the bars that move into the level versus those that leave the level. If the bars leaving the level are bigger and cover more ground, this is a good indication of how strong the level is.

In addition to the size, make sure you tie the strength evaluation into the overall context as well. For example, in Figure 6, the final swing point where the bullish engulfing bar exists is a really strong swing point. At this point in time, we know that the bears are asserting themselves.

For prices to swing upwards in this manner at such a steep angle and with bars being as large as they are, we have an indication that the extent to which price will likely move will be large.

Repeatedly Tested Levels

You've just learned that sideways moves are not swing points. However, they are a valid form of support or resistance. This is because levels that are repeatedly tested by prices are an indicator that traders are present at that level. Much like with swing points, the angles that form off these levels and the distance that prices move from them are an indication of how strong they are.

The larger the sideways move is, the stronger the level will be. In addition to this, levels that have large gaps between retests are stronger than ones that have small gaps. This makes sense because a level that is tested and retested with a large gap in between indicates that traders are willing to hang around at that level for a long time.

This means when prices retest the level for a third time, it's more likely than not that they'll be present. Keep in mind that a retest alone doesn't indicate strength. You need to examine the quality of the bounces that the level is producing.

If you notice that the bounces off a resistance level become smaller in size and that the size of the bars after the retests are shrinking in size, then this indicates that the level is becoming weaker. Often in the FX markets, you'll see weak bounces followed by strong ones which can be confusing to trade.

However, in the crypto market, this doesn't occur very often thanks to the lower competition and volumes that exist. It just makes it that much easier to trade crypto.

Prior Reaction Zones

Areas that have witnessed huge price reactions in the past indicate that there are traders present there who are willing to push prices back the other way.

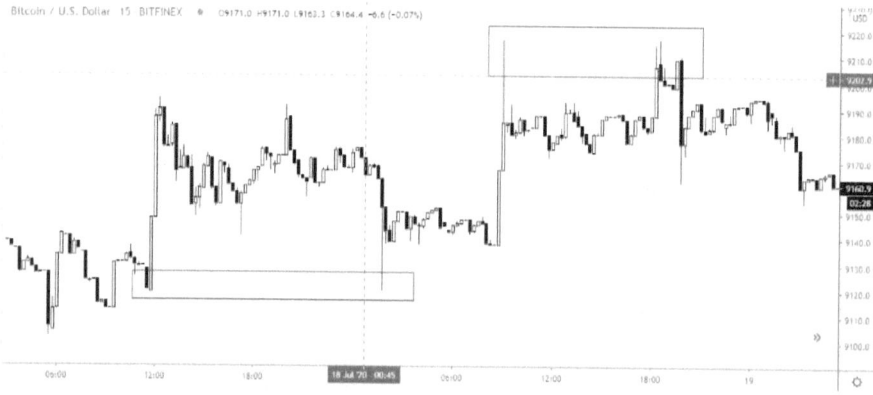

Figure 7: Prior Reaction Zones

Figure 7 shows two zones where prices reacted by a large degree before they were retested. The first box shows a strong bullish reaction. Notice the size of the bullish bars leaving this level. Notice that when prices retest this level they do so through a bearish bar.

Not only do the bulls at this level manage to push prices back up and create a tail, they manage to push them even higher after a brief sideways move.

The second box on top shows how the bears managed to temper the price rise. Two strong bullish bars are met with resistance from the bears. After prices retreat the first time, it retests the level but the bears move back in and push prices down. This particular chart shows a context that is extremely concentrated in terms of bullish and bearish pressure.

Both sides of the market are very close to one another. This produces volatility. However, given the sideways nature of the market, you can see how easy it is to enter and exit within a very small range and make a profit.

Higher Time Frames

When day trading, you'll be operating somewhere between the five-minute charts to the one-hour charts. All of these time frames have higher time frames that exist above them. For example, the higher time frame when trading a 30-minute chart is the hourly chart. For the hourly, it's the daily, and so on.

Levels and zones that exist on those higher time frames are especially strong on the time frame you're operating in. For example, if you're trading the 15-minute chart and see prices make a V-shaped bottom or top, and then move in the other direction, this means it's probably hit a higher time frame level.

To understand why this happens, you need to know that traders exist on every time frame. There are traders on your time frame, on the one below yours, and on the one above yours. The higher time frames tend to produce longer lasting effects because the trends and ranges (their contexts) last for longer.

As a result, they overrule any price action that occurs on the lower time frames. This is also why you must be very conscious of where the higher time frame levels are and what their context is when placing your trades. You might spot a strong uptrend on the lower time frame but if it's going to run into a strong level on the higher time frame, then your trade isn't going anywhere.

This brings to a close our look at support and resistance levels. Above all else, remember that these areas are zones despite the word "level" being attached to them. They won't be clean and horizontal. In fact, they'll be like the boxes I drew in the previous chart. If you do find a zone that conforms to a horizontal line, then this is a good thing.

Cleaner ones like this allow you to place your stop losses closer, which means your trade doesn't have to move as far to earn a profit. When it comes to determining the extent of wider zones, look for the areas that prices have bounced off the most. The bounciest areas within a zone are where the most traders are present.

When combining support and resistance analysis with trend/range analysis, you'll be able to fully trade without the assistance of price action patterns. You'll be able to simply enter at the level no matter what the price looks like and place a stop loss away from the zone.

Trading in this manner requires you to have a lot of skill, both in technical as well as mental terms. However, it's something that can be learned through practice and repetition. When starting off, you can rely on price action patterns and on indicators (which you'll learn in the next chapter); however, always practice trading this way.

Day Trading Cryptocurrency

If you can trade in this manner, you'll be trading price action directly and you won't have to worry about an indicator losing its effectiveness. Above all else, let go of the need to be right on every single trade and you'll find that profits will come to you easily.

Chapter 6: Indicators

When starting out, many traders use indicators to help them make sense of the market. This is a good thing because indicators can simplify a lot of complex price action. However, in the long run, it's best to move away from them. There are a few indicators that work very well and are evergreen. They tend to provide a wide variety of signals.

The flip side is that they also tend to waver in terms of efficiency. Sometimes, you'll find that one type of signal is extremely effective, while at other times another type is. This sort of variation is normal with indicators and it makes money management extremely important.

There are also indicators that are self-contained trading systems unto themselves. These are more reliable because they provide you with easy-to-decipher entry and exit systems. The problem with these indicators is that traders often get too smart with them and in the name of optimizing them, tend to sabotage themselves.

This chapter is going to give you both types of indicators. Keep in mind that some of them work better when combined with the lessons of the previous two chapters, while some can be used by themselves in a standalone manner. You can even combine price action patterns with them to increase their efficiency.

With all indicators, it's important to spend some time testing how well they work for you. The thing with indicators is that they always work. Whether they work for you depends on your mental makeup. Some traders work better with certain indicators than others. The testing phase will help you figure out which ones work best for you.

Another thing to keep in mind is that no indicator is going to be perfect. Many struggling traders continue to struggle because they think their results will get better if they have better indicators. They jump around all the time, changing their system, and as a result, don't allow their system to make them money.

Sometimes, this behavior presents itself as tweaking the numbers associated with indicators. Every indicator requires an input and some people obsess over finding the perfect number that will give them a win every single time. If trading was a matter of finding the right number, then everyone would be a successful trader.

The real way to make money in trading is to figure out the odds of your system and then manage your money in such a way that your capital keeps growing. It requires you to think in counterintuitive ways, as you'll see in the next chapter.

So as you read about these indicators, don't get carried away thinking they're perfect or that you can tweak them to be perfect. All of them will provide wins for a certain amount of time and losses the rest of the time. It's your job to figure out how often this occurs and to structure a risk management strategy that allows you to come out ahead despite this win/loss profile.

Bollinger Bands

The first indicator you're going to learn about is a self-contained trading system. In fact, there are two trading systems that are inherent to Bollinger bands and both of them are equally effective. You can ignore the trend-versus-range analysis when using them. However, as you'll see, the trading systems are far more effective if you can perform a simple analysis.

Bollinger bands have been around for a long time now, and they continue to be effective. One of the reasons for this is their simplicity. The bands are plotted as envelopes that surround price. Here's how they're constructed: The 20-period average of the price closes is plotted to form a 20-period exponential moving average (EMA) curve.

This sounds complicated but it is actually quite simple. The average closing prices of the previous 20 bars is calculated and is plotted on the chart. These plots are connected together (since the 20-period range will keep changing as the chart moves forward) and a curve is formed.

Some representations of the Bollinger bands show this curve while some don't. It isn't important either way. From this EMA, a curve that is three standard deviations away is plotted above and below. These three standard deviations or "three sigma" curves are the Bollinger bands. They represent the extremes of possible price movement.

Why is three sigma chosen and not six or seven? You can tinker with this input in your trading software. However, three is universally accepted as being an extreme movement in the markets.

Day Trading Cryptocurrency

Figure 8: Bollinger Bands

Figure 8 illustrates what the Bollinger bands look like when plotted on a chart. In this chart, I've marked certain points with rectangles and circles. Both of these indicate entry points depending on your strategy of choice. Let's look at the circles first.

The circles indicate what is called a "mean reversion strategy" and this is a profitable one in sideways-moving markets. When markets are moving in a certain range, any hit on the outer envelope will usually result in price moving away from it since it's at an extreme level.

Notice that the circles indicate areas where prices hit one of the outer envelopes. If prices hit the lower envelope, you would go long (buy), and if they hit the upper envelope, you would short (sell). Ride prices all the way back down to the bottom envelope and close your trade out for a profit.

If the envelope is big enough, you could even wait for prices to reach the EMA that runs through the middle of the envelopes and exit your trades there. Looking at the number of circles on the chart, you can see that this is a pretty active trading strategy. You'll be jumping in and out of the markets quite a lot.

Not all of these entries will result in a profit. Some of them will go for losses. Also, notice how this strategy does not work when the market moves into a downtrend. In those times, prices hug the bottom envelope but don't recover. This is normal because in a trend, one side of the market is extremely imbalanced.

If you could read the price action context to figure out that the market is about to enter a downtrend, then you'd be able to stay away from trading this strategy in a trend. You could also simply look at the market and if it's printing larger bars in a given direction, you could reason that a trend is about to begin and simply stay away from it.

As the market settles back into a range after the downtrend, notice how prices move in a mean reversion pattern once again. The minute they hit one of the outer envelopes, they make it back to the EMA at the very least.

The way to trade this strategy would be to enter the minute prices hit one of the outer envelopes and place a stop some distance away from your entry. Take your exit either at the moment prices reach the other envelope, or when they pass the EMA. The former exit will result in more profit but you'll win a smaller percentage of your trades. The latter will result in smaller profits but it's more likely to give you a win.

That's the first strategy. It's an extremely short term strategy even from a day trading perspective. You'll be in a trade for a few bars at the most. The chart shown above is a 15-minute one and most trades last for three or four bars at the most. The second strategy is one that keeps you in a trade for a lot longer and it results in greater profits.

However, the possibility of loss is also increased. This strategy is the Bollinger band squeeze. A squeeze occurs when the bands contract towards one another and then explode away from each other. You'll notice these points by looking at the rectangles in the chart.

At these points, the bands come close to one another and then move away from each other. What does this signify? Given that the bands are a measure of the standard deviation of price movement, they can be seen as a measure of volatility. As a day trader, your task is to enter during moments of low volatility and exit during moments of high volatility.

This way, you can enter when prices are in a narrow band and exit once they've moved sharply in a given direction. The squeeze indicates that one side of the market is taking over and is ready to push prices in a given direction. Think of it as a loaded spring that is compressed. If you compress it enough, it'll eventually explode forcefully.

From the chart above, you can see that prices move in a given direction after the squeeze. The moves might not be explosive at all times but there's no denying that prices acquire a directional bent to them. Crucially, the squeeze allows you to spot the downtrend which would have made you a ton of money had you captured it.

The squeeze is a tougher strategy to trade from a mental standpoint. There will be times when you'll think the bands are squeezing and prices won't move explosively enough for you to make any money. There's also the fact that you'll need to figure out which direction to place your trade in. The bands let you know that a move is coming but they don't tell you which way prices are going to move. Simple trend/range analysis will tell you this.

This strategy works well in times where a trend is coming to an end and you find yourself in a large range that commonly occurs at the end of it. In the range that occurs after the downtrend, you can see that it's not as effective. This is the initial portion of a large range and the bears still have some say in how prices move.

Thus, the reactions aren't as strong as you'd expect. Over time, the bulls will assert themselves but as of now, this isn't happening. The flip side is that despite the low success rate of the squeeze, you'll end up making many multiples of how much you lose on average during the times when you do make money.

Thus, risk management is extremely important when it comes to this strategy. This also ties into why this is a tough strategy to trade from a mental perspective.

EMA Crossovers

The EMA crossover is a simple strategy that most traders discount. Ironically, they discount it precisely because it's so simple. It's a strategy that still produces results when traded in the stock markets and in FX. In the crypto markets, it's even more effective thanks to many traders simply refusing to use it.

This is a strategy that requires you to understand how a trend is developing. Much like candlestick patterns, you'll need to filter signals in order to be successful. Some signals might not make sense for you to trade while some will be valid. It depends on the environment that is prevalent at the time.

Ranges usually don't lend themselves well to crossover strategies. During these times, prices are non-directional and you'll see that many crossovers occur. However, in trending markets, this strategy works really well.

A crossover occurs when one element crosses another. In this case, a crossover refers to when an EMA crosses another EMA that has a different lookback period. For example, if the five-period EMA crosses the 20-period EMA, this is a crossover. The direction of the crossover determines the direction you will place your trade in.

Figure 9: EMA Crossover

Day Trading Cryptocurrency

In Figure 9, you can see an example of how powerful a crossover strategy can be. The stepped line indicates the five-period EMA, while the regular line is the 20-period EMA. The chart is the 15-minute time frame in Bitcoin.

When the five-EMA crosses below the 20 EMA, this is an indication that the immediate price movement is trending downwards as compared to the previous price action. This means a downswing can be expected. The smaller period's EMA is also referred to as the faster EMA because of this. It simply reacts more quickly to price changes.

The great thing about a crossover strategy is that it gives you the direction of the trade entry. If the five-EMA crosses from below to above the slower EMA, then you'll need to enter a bullish trade. However, just because a crossover occurs doesn't mean you should enter. Take care to observe the price action context and trade accordingly.

Stick to environments that are already trending and stay away from ranges. In the chart above, prices are already trending slightly and are about to accelerate downwards. This is why the crossover works so well and almost every entry produces a profit.

You can enter on the close of the bar that occurs after the crossover with a stop either above that bar or above/below a relevant support or resistance level. In case the trend accelerates, you can let the trade run and collect your profits according to your risk management rules, as I'll explain in the next chapter.

In ranging environments, you'll find that there will be a lot of crossovers, making this strategy limited in that sense. Unlike the Bollinger bands, this isn't an all-weather strategy. The good news is that you can use simple support and resistance trading techniques to trade ranges. Go long at range bottoms and short at the range tops. Given that the range boundaries tend to be quite strong in terms of support and resistance, you'll find that prices will move to the other boundary like clockwork.

Thus, combining your knowledge of trend/range analysis with the crossover will result in a profitable strategy.

Chapter 7: Risk Management

One of the most critical things for your trading success is risk management. Unfortunately, most traders ignore this aspect of trading and pursue increasingly-complex technical analysis strategies. While your technical skills are important, they're just a piece of the puzzle.

A simple trading strategy can make you money as long as you have excellent risk management. The reason most traders don't take risk into account is because of a flawed understanding with regards to how trading works. Ask yourself this question: While reading the previous chapters on technical analysis, how often did you think that a strategy would give you a 100% success rate?

Here's another way of thinking about it: If you were presented with a strategy that had a 99% success rate and another that had a 30% success rate, which would you rate as being better? Odds are that you'd pick the former system as being better. However, this is incorrect.

The truth is that you don't have enough information to make a decision. Understanding why this is cuts to the heart of risk management.

Understanding Risk

Day Trading Cryptocurrency

The markets are an extremely random environment. In the short term, you're trying to predict prices that are influenced by human emotion. The prices you see on your screen are influenced by what traders think of that asset at any given point in time. There's no predicting human emotions.

Consider how difficult it is to predict how someone close to you will react to an event. You might be able to predict their reaction with reasonable accuracy, but will you be able to predict it 100% accurately all the time? This is unlikely. When it comes to the market, you're dealing with millions of traders who you'll never lay eyes on.

This is why successful trading is all about reading which way the market is already moving and then jumping on board. It isn't about trying to position yourself at the front of the line. The traders who try to do this are effectively trying to predict human emotions and, more often than not, they end up making a loss.

Instead, you need to accept the clues that the market gives you and then ride it in the direction it moves in. The next thing to realize is that despite doing this, your technical system isn't going to put you in the best position at all times. There will be times when you'll receive a false positive signal and this will cause you to lose money.

Thus, relying on a system that has a high success rate as its sole calling card does not make sense. This is because a high success rate does not imply that you can make money. A system might predict the direction of the market correctly. However, the market might not move enough for you to be able to make a profit.

Consider a case where you're calling the flip of a coin with a friend. You know that the odds of a head landing are 50%. What are the odds of you correctly calling the next coin flip, though? Would you bet money with someone over a single coin flip? Put it in another way: Is it better for you to bet on the outcome of a single coin flip or a million coin flips?

If you were paid double every time you called correctly, a million flips is always the better option. This is because you know that in over a million flips, the coin will most likely land heads at least 500,000 times. If you bet over a single flip, you don't stand any chance of making money. At the very least, your success depends entirely on luck.

For over a million flips though, it isn't luck. It's just working out the probabilities. Notice that your success in this scenario depends on two factors: The odds of a head landing is 50% and you're getting paid twice more than what you would lose when you call incorrectly.

Trading is similar. Traders who focus on developing high success rate systems are effectively trying to chase a system where they can call a head or a tail accurately 100% of the time. Successful traders instead accept that the odds are 50% and then develop ways to get paid more when they call correctly as opposed to how much they lose when they're incorrect.

Thus, you need to focus on maintaining the relationship between two metrics in your trading: The success rate of your system and the amount of money you win versus how much you lose on average.

Win Rate

The win rate of your system is simply how many times your trades result in you making money. If you make money six times out of 10, then your win rate is 60%. In most of the things we deal with in our lives, the win rate is all that matters. Consider the education systems we were raised in.

Answer enough questions correctly and you'll end up scoring a high grade. This high grade allows you to progress through the system. However, this is not how many systems in the real world work. How many times have you seen a person work half as hard as you, know less than you, and still get paid more?

This is because while you were focusing on being right most of the time, they were focused on being right enough and gaining a bigger advantage when they were right as opposed to when they were wrong. A casino works on the same principle.

When a player places a bet on one of their games, the casino stands to lose money. Every game has certain odds and these are stacked in favor of the house. Some games have million-dollar jackpots and the casino stands to lose this money if the player calls their hand correctly.

The casino doesn't mind losing this money, though. All they're focused on is making sure the winner plays enough hands. This is because the more hands they play, the greater the chances of the odds of that game asserting itself. This means that the casino will eventually win its money back. It's why you'll see casinos encouraging players to bet all of their winnings back into the game with the promise of winning more.

The player does this and ends up donating their winnings right back to the house. Thanks to the way their odds are set up, it's virtually impossible to lose money running a casino.

Risk-Reward Ratio

This ratio is the second metric that you must pay attention to. Your win rate is important, but how much of a multiple of your risk are you making every time you're right? Put another way, are you really driving home your advantage when you're right? The amount of money you risk per trade should be your average loss amount. Typically, this is denoted by the variable R. When you're right about the market, how much of a multiple of R are you making?

Let's say you have a system that is correct 50% of the time. If your winning multiple is 0.5R (half of your risk per trade), you're not going to make money in the long run. Consider a small 10 trade sample. Over this period, you'll lose five trades for a loss of -5R.

You'll win five trades for a profit of 2.5R. This leaves you with a -2.5R loss. However, if your win multiple was 2.5R, you'd be making a lot of money. This multiple is often referred to as the "risk-reward ratio".

Technically, the order of those words should be flipped but in trading circles this is how it's often referred to. Together with your win rate, you need to make sure this ratio lines up to create a scenario where you can be profitable.

Trading profitability is thus not a linear thing where the more often you're right, the more money you'll make. Instead, it's a band that varies depending on what your risk-reward ratio is along with your win rate. You can be profitable being right just 20% of the time and you can make losses being right 95% of the time.

The Bollinger band squeeze system highlighted previously is an example of how a low win rate system can make a lot of money when the risk-reward ratio is high. When you catch a big trend with that system, your win amount is going to be extremely high compared to your average loss.

This realization means there are a few simple principles you must follow in order to be successful at trading.

Successful Principles

Follow these risk management principles and you'll find that you'll manage to make money no matter what sort of conditions are present in the market.

Risk the Same Amount Every Trade

It's crucial for you to risk the same amount of money every single trade you take. This is what keeps your risk-reward ratio consistent. Don't be misled by the word "amount". I'm not talking about fixing a sum of money to risk all the time. Instead, fix your risk per trade to a certain percentage of your account balance.

As your account grows, this amount will grow along with it. Since your exits are at a multiple of risk that ensures you'll be profitable over time, your average win will line up with your average loss. This is how you can guarantee that your account will grow the more you trade.

How much should you risk per trade? When starting out, you should not be risking more than 0.5% of your account. This looks like a small amount of money but it's what makes your survival more probable. You've read the statistics of day traders in the market. Make no mistake, during the first year of trading, your aim should be to survive and preserve your capital as much as possible.

Once you get past that first year, you can then focus on increasing your risk per trade and making more money.

Track

How can you make sure you're risking the correct amount of money every trade and are taking your rewards at the correct exit points all the time? Well, this is where journaling comes into the picture. You should jot down all information pertaining to your trading, including the entry price, the stop-loss level, the risk you took on the trade, and the reason for entry.

The same applies on the exit as well. Make sure you take screenshots of your trade entry and exit. Review your trades once a week to make sure you're sticking to your rules. It's also a good idea to record your screen during the session to get a deeper look at what you're doing in real time.

Day Trading Cryptocurrency

Test

Before jumping into live trading, you need to spend some time figuring out what the risk numbers of your system look like. What is its win rate and what is the average win amount versus the average loss? The best way to do this is to paper trade or demo trade.

Demo trading is a slower process that will take you close to six months to collect enough relevant data for your trades. I mention six months because this is a long enough period for day traders to place enough trades and to evaluate how their system works.

You can also choose to simulate your trades on a software program. As of current writing, there isn't any program that allows you to replay historical cryptocurrency data, unfortunately. However, you can simulate your system on a software like Forextester or Ninjatrader, which will give you data on how it performs in stocks and FX.

It'll also allow you to practice your skills and get better at trading your system. Once you've collected enough data (at least 200 trades), run the numbers and look at where you can improve your system. Can you increase your win amount? Can you increase your win rate?

Will decreasing your win rate result in you making more money? Ask yourself all of these questions and tinker with your system. Once you have a system finalized, trade it live and stick to your rules no matter what.

Practice

It's important for you to set aside time to practice your skills to the point where you can automatically execute your system. The live-trading environment is fast paced and your emotions will be running haywire. It's understandable because money is involved. We get intensely emotional about money since it's something that is deeply connected to our identities.

To mitigate this and the risk of you doing something out of an emotionally-driven reason, you should practice your skills when you aren't trading live. Repeat executing your skills often enough and your system will ingrain itself in your brain.

In conclusion, practice good risk management principles and ally them to a technical system that you can understand and execute well. Follow the steps of your system in an orderly manner and you'll find yourself making money easily.

Conclusion

Cryptocurrencies pose immense opportunities for the savvy trader. However, to take advantage of them, you need to trade smart. Many traders think that success is a function of merely working hard. They think that the more trades they place, the more money they'll make.

This is partially true. What really matters is that you place trades that are relevant to your strategy. Placing trades just for the heck of it won't make you any money. In fact, it'll only make you an involuntary donor in the market. Do not underestimate the impact your emotions will have on you when you begin trading.

They will cause you to overtrade or seek revenge on the markets by trying to recover the money you lost previously. The best way to keep these emotions in check is to journal your trades and to always keep your rules in mind. By enforcing your rules and by becoming conscious of when you're about to break them, you'll manage to stay on the right side of your risk management plan.

There are a few terms and concepts about cryptocurrencies you'll need to learn prior to trading them, such as wallets, the blockchain, and so on. However, once you're past this hurdle, trading them is the same as with any other instrument. You'll need to follow the same principles that will bring you day trading success in the stock and FX market.

In the crypto market, you're more likely to gain success because the level of competition you face is lower. Thus, you'll be able to gain more bang for your buck, so to speak. There will be people who will tell you that the volatility in cryptos is far too high. However, this volatility is what helps you make money in the long run.

Make sure you place your stop losses at a good distance away from your order entry levels. This will help you account for the additional volatility that these instruments have. Always keep your risk per trade consistent and follow sound technical trading principles.

Over the long run, it's better for you to trade without the aid of indicators or candlestick patterns. Trading by reading the trend/range distribution and the support and resistance levels will help you get close to the order flow and you'll be able to predict the direction of price in a much better way.

Best of all, you'll never have to worry about an indicator becoming irrelevant or a system losing its potency. Order flow is what creates price action patterns and other indicators, so by deciphering it directly, you'll always remain up-to-date with what the market is doing.

Day Trading Cryptocurrency

Something that helps traders maintain their profits is to establish a fixed routine day-in and day-out. Following the same routine will help train your mind in the ways that you need it to behave when in the markets. This will help you avoid costly mistakes that most other traders make.

Take your trading seriously and don't expect to roll out of bed and instantly be able to trade well. That's not how it works. Prepare for the markets like you would any serious work-related task and you'll find that profits will come to you.

I wish you the best of luck and all the profits in the world with your trading. It's a tough endeavor but one that is immensely rewarding.

Till then, happy trading!

References

Antonopoulos, A. M., & O'Reilly Media. (2018). *Mastering Bitcoin : programming the open blockchain*. O'Reilly.

Saifedean Ammous. (2018). *The Bitcoin standard : the decentralized alternative to central banking*. John Wiley & Sons, Inc.

Investopedia. (2019). *What is the gold standard?* https://www.investopedia.com/ask/answers/09/gold-standard.asp